Enter in Peace

Enter in Peace

The Doorways of Cairo Homes
1872–1950

Ahmed Abdel-Gawad

With photographs by the author

The American University in Cairo Press
Cairo • New York

Copyright © 2007 by
The American University in Cairo Press
113 Sharia Kasr el Aini, Cairo, Egypt
420 Fifth Avenue, New York, NY 10018
www.aucpress.com

Map on page viii by Ola Seif.

Photograph in plate 88 by Emile Béchard, c. 1880, courtesy of the Rare Books and
Special Collections Library, the American University in Cairo.

Dar el Kutub No. 15644/06
ISBN 978 977 416 062 2

1 2 3 4 5 6   12 11 10 09 08 07

Designed by Sally Boylan/AUC Press Design Center
Printed in Egypt

CONTENTS

I would like to express my sincere gratitude to Dr. Karim Castel for his fruitful idea and for his support in producing this work. I am greatly indebted to architect Muhammad Abu al-Amaiem for his help and encouragement. I would also like to thank Mrs. Yousriya Hamed and Ms. Giehan Fouad for their assistance in the artwork for this book.

PREFACE

An integral architectural element of buildings, doorways have long held special significance in Muslim societies, where homes are entered with the greeting, *al-salam alaykum*— 'peace be upon you.' Years ago it was customary in Egypt to inscribe on doorway lintels the Qur'anic inscription, "Enter in peace."

The design and decorative character of Cairo doorways are patterned on the buildings' architectural style, but greatly affected by prevailing social, economic, and political influences. Twentieth-century doors are mainly characterized by serpent and crescent designs. Predominant in Cairo's old districts, these two decorative units are a reflection of the nationalist movement brought by the 1919 Revolution.

Studies of architectural and decorative elements found in Cairo's nineteenth- and early twentieth-century buildings deal primarily with the Cairo of Khedive Isma'il: the newer quarters of the city. This study focuses on the doorways of houses built in Cairo's older neighborhoods during that and the following period. Of the eighty-one doors and their façades presented here in photographs, the oldest dates to AH 1289 / AD 1872. The dimensions of these doorways and their various elements are described, along with records of the house owner and construction date collected from Egypt's public tax records and other sources.

CENTRAL CAIRO

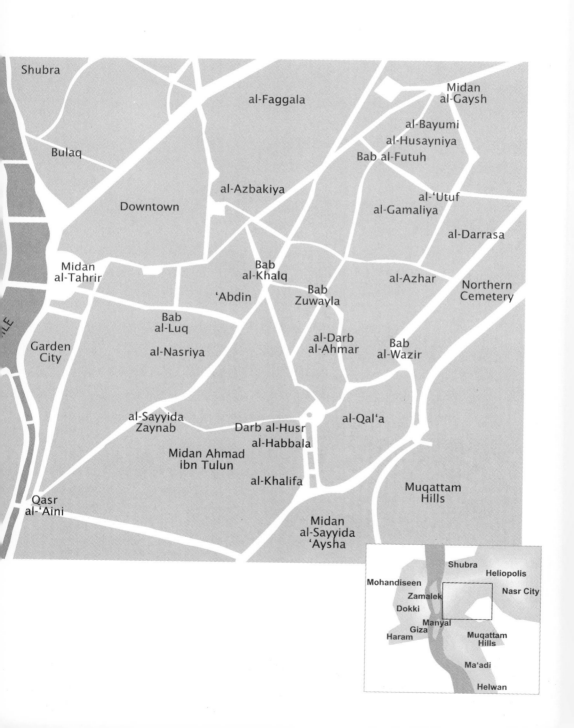

Shubra

al-Faggala

Midan
al-Gaysh

al-Bayumi
al-Husayniya
Bab al-Futuh

Bulaq

al-Azbakiya

Downtown

al-'Utuf
al-Gamaliya

al-Darrasa

Midan
al-Tahrir

Bab
al-Khalq

al-Azhar

Northern
Cemetery

'Abdin

Bab
Zuwayla

Bab
al-Luq

Garden
City

al-Nasriya

al-Darb
al-Ahmar

Bab
al-Wazir

al-Sayyida
Zaynab

Darb al-Husr
al-Habbala

al-Qal'a

Midan Ahmad
ibn Tulun

al-Khalifa

Qasr
al-'Aini

Muqattam
Hills

Midan
al-Sayyida
'Aysha

Shubra
Heliopolis

Mohandiseen

Zamalek

Nasr City

Dokki

Manyal
Giza
Haram

Muqattam
Hills

Ma'adi

Helwan

INTRODUCTION

D oors and entrances, together called 'doorways,' are important
elements in the architecture of the Arab and Islamic worlds. In
Cairo, doors are an integral part of the entrances of both religious structures, such as mosques, *khanqah*s, and *tikiya*s, and secular
buildings such as public baths, street fountains, khans, hospitals, schools,
and residential dwellings.

Faith adds a dimension to architecture. Apart from rituals, Islam is a
way of life, where the inward spiritual condition of the human being and the
external environment are interdependent. This homogeneity between body
and soul—the material and the spiritual—has its expression rooted in the
tradition, or *sunna*, of the Prophet Muhammad. The *sunna* counsels on the
simplest of human activities, such as how to behave within the family and
toward a stranger, the receiving of a guest, neighborliness, the extended
family, and so on. Thus, the *sunna* indirectly fashions all aspects of life,
including the home, community, and architecture.[1]

According to the commandment of *al-Sunna al-nabawiya* (the
Prophetic traditions), religious scholar Ibn al-Hagg (d. AH 737 / AD 1336)
explains that when a trader returns home from his travels, he should send
someone ahead to inform his family of his homecoming. The *sunna* pro-
hibits a traveler from unexpectedly returning home in the middle of the

night or arriving without warning, denying his family the chance to prepare for his return.²

As the *sunna* determines all aspects of human activities in accordance with tradition, it represents the norms of ideal behavior. This also goes for material things. The construction of buildings and the type of decoration are also determined by the *sunna*. To those who said the buildings of our forebears were different from later buildings, Ibn al-Hagg's response was that many of the building in his time were small and narrow, like those built by his predecessors.³ The best way of building, according to the commandment of the *sunna*, is to abide by tradition.

Islamic culture pays particular attention to the privacy and sanctity of one's home. *Al-Sunna al-nabawiya* committed Muslims to enter the house from its proper doorway following the commandment, *Idkhulu al-buyut min abwabiha*. Visitors in Muslim societies are obliged to seek the occupants' permission to enter, announcing themselves with the greeting, *al-salam alaykum*. From medieval times to the twentieth century, the Qur'anic verse from Surat al-Hijr 46, *Idkhuluha bi-salamin aminin* ('Enter in peace and security'), was inscribed on the lintels of both religious and secular buildings, hence the particular importance of doorways in Egypt's buildings.

In traditional urban Islamic societies, buildings and their doorways reflect both a utilitarian and a spiritual vision, and Cairo doorways of the nineteenth and twentieth centuries are clear examples of this synthesis. The doorways of houses and other structures built for the middle classes in Egypt received special attention, architecturally and decoratively, from their builders and owners. Typical doorways of buildings constructed during the second half of the nineteenth century and at the dawn of the twentieth century can still be found in Cairo's older quarters, such as al-Darrasa, al-Darb al-Ahmar, Bab al-Wazir, al-Qal'a, and Bulaq, and also in the more modern districts of Shubra, al-Azbakiya, Midan al-Tahrir, al-Faggala, Garden City, Zamalek, and Heliopolis.

Figure 1: Early nineteenth-century doorway.

During the period considered here for its architectural examples, Egyptians experienced rapid and far-reaching political and economic changes, which also altered patterns of social mobility, affecting especially the middle classes, the artisans, and the professionals. It is their residences that are of particular interest in this photographic survey, rather than the apartment buildings, villas, and palaces of Egypt's upper classes in the districts of Garden City, Zamalek, Heliopolis, Ma'adi, al-Azbakiya, al-Tahrir, and Bab al-Luq, which became residential districts exclusively for the wealthy in the early twentieth century. The doorways and the façades of many of these buildings still stand, revealing features of the architectural and religious conventions of the Egyptians who owned and built them.

Cairo, a History of Two Cities

In the Ottoman period, 1517 to 1798 (the year of the Napoleonic conquest), the major change in the city of Cairo was its expansion westward across the Khalig al-Masri from Fatimid Cairo in the east to the newly developed port of Bulaq northwest of the old city.[4] Beginning in the tenth century, during Fatimid rule, walls were built around Cairo. While originally defensive in nature, the city grew within these walls until its increasing population led to expansion beyond the walls. A seventeenth-century document notes that wealthy residents occupied the greater part of the Cairo area within the walls with the exception of the quarters to the east that were nevertheless close to the walls (Qasr al-Shuq, al-Batliya, al-'Utuf). Some districts situated south of Bab Zuwayla and outside the city walls, such as those near al-Salah Tala'i' Mosque, the al-Qirabiya, and al-Dawidiya, were also occupied by wealthier residents. The areas occupied by the poor, located at the city's borders, were located in the eastward quarters, to the southeast of Cairo (Darb Shughlan), south of the city (al-Habala, al-Hataba, Qala'at al-Kabsh), to the west (Bab al-Luq, al-Manasra, al-Fawala), and in the north (districts situated outside al-Husayniya). The areas occupied by middle-class citizens consisted of all the districts situated between the wealthy and the poorer areas.[5]

During the eighteenth century, there were no substantial changes in the demographics of the city despite its considerable expansion: patterns of large and small property holdings closely match those of the seventeenth century. After describing the city's various quarters as comprising wealthy, middle-class, or poorer dwellings, social historian Nelly Hanna finds that between the years 1738 and 1744, some 60 percent of the homes of wealthy persons were located in what were considered wealthy quarters, 40 percent of such houses were in essentially middle-class areas, and none were located in the poorer districts. Of the city's two hundred middle-class houses, 28 percent were in wealthy districts, 60 percent in middle-class districts, and 12 percent in poorer districts. Of 357 modest homes, 14 percent were in the wealthy quarters, 56 percent in the middle-class quarters, and 30 percent in the poorer areas.[6] This intermingling of large and small holdings in all three types of residential quarters—predominantly wealthy, middle-class, or poor—reflected the intermingling of owners and residents of varying social and economic levels.

Interspersed among the mansions and residences of the wealthy are the modest houses of middle-class craftsmen or artisans and traders, with floor space ranging from 147 to 380 square meters. Consider the neighbors of these middle-class dwellings: Bayt al-Suhaymi with 2,500 square meters in the middle-class district of al-Darb al-Asfar, al-Gamaliya; the Musafir Khana with 1,257 square meters in al-Gamaliya; and the Jamal al-Din al-Dhahabi house with 718 square meters in Khush Kadam, Shari' al-Mu'izz.[7]

During the reigns of Muhammad 'Ali (1805–1849) and Khedive Isma'il (1863–1879), no fundamental changes took place in the distribution of holdings inside the older Cairo districts. Houses of wealthy pashas and beys had adjoined modest and poor houses in approximately the same pattern since the seventeenth century. Indeed, in the last third of the nineteenth century, there are several examples of large buildings with floor areas of 600 to 1,300 square meters side by side with buildings of only 90 to 300 square meters of floor space. The larger residences were built by ministry officials and senior civil servants, leading personalities, scholars, and wealthy merchants, while the smaller dwellings were owned by white-collar workers, low-ranking officials, lawyers, and traders. A prominent example of this class intermingling is the area around 55 Shari' Bab al-Wazir (plate 7). The building at 2 Shari' Bayn al-Sayarig (plate 75) in the Bab al-Sha'riya district is no larger than 90 square meters (author's measurement).

Shari' Bab al-Wazir and its extension on both sides of Shari' al-Tabana in the Bab Zuwayla quarter and Shari' al-Mahgar in al-Qal'a quarter show many large buildings once inhabited by senior civil servants and governors holding the title of pasha interspersed with middle-class residences. The estate on 55 Shari' Bab al-Wazir (plate 7) was the property of the heirs of Isma'il Pasha Siddiq and Muhammad Bey Tawfik.[8] Isma'il Pasha Siddiq (1821–1876) was one of Egypt's leading statesmen during the reign of Khedive Isma'il. Next door, 53 Shari' Bab al-Wazir was the property of 'Abd al-Hamid Pasha Sadiq,[9] and adjacent number 51 was the property of Sadiq's daughters, Fatma Hanem and Munira Hanem. Hassan Pasha Madkur and his brothers owned the property at 13 Shari' al-Tabana.[10] Other large residences in this quarter, such as 25 Darb al-Qazzazin, Shari' Bab al-Wazir (plate 1), may be recognized by their architectural styles as dating to the first quarter of the nineteenth century.

The juxtaposition of middle-class and upper-class residences was not restricted to Shari' Bab al-Wazir and its extensions. Midan Ahmad ibn Tulun, where smaller, middle-class dwellings predominated, was also the address of residents with the title of bey. An example is 25 Shari' Ahmad ibn Tulun (plate 16), built in 1900, which was the property of the heirs of Muhammad Bey Mahdi.[11] Two other homes in this district, 18 Sikkat al-Mahgar (plate 8), with the construction date of AH 1291 / AD 1874 recorded on the door, and 29 Darb al-Habbala (plate 29), dated AH 1292 / AD 1875, are notable examples of smaller, middle-class residences.

In addition to the houses in old Cairo belonging to statesmen and senior civil servants with the title of pasha or bey, there are large residences owned by lesser-known people. Some were the homes of wealthy merchants such as that at 1 Raba' al-Ruz in Bulaq (AH 1295 / AD 1878) (plate 21), became the property of Hassan al-Kafrawy's heirs.[12] Some belonged to the Turkish or Circassian communities who lived in Egypt. An example of a nineteenth-century dwelling is 20 Shari' al-'Umrany (plate 14), the property of Su'ad Hanem al-Sharkasiya.[13]

During Khedive Isma'il's reign the city expanded westward with the construction in 1868 of a new quarter named Isma'iliya at the edge of al-Azbakiya Gardens. The expansion of the western quarters became the nucleus of a 'new' Cairo, which differed greatly from old Cairo in terms of demography, types of owners, and the social classes inhabiting these areas. Since then the newly built areas of Cairo have followed European architectural styles.

In contrast to the old city, "where the majority of lands were owned by thousands," private lands in the modern extensions of the city were owned by fewer than one hundred individuals or their heirs.[14] In 1892, the quarters extending between the railway station in the west and the Khalig in the east, and between Qasr al-'Ayni and Garden City to the south, and al-Faggala and al-Zahir in the north, "were owned by persons with the titles of pasha, bey, or effendi. Together, these owners possessed three-quarters of the land previously owned by individuals."[15] Pashas were among the most important landowners in the Isma'iliya quarter. Half of the population of beys, representing the second category in the Egyptian administrative structure, was centered in the limited areas of Bab al-Luq and Midan al-Nasriya. The owners of minor possessions, the effendis, representing the largest middle-class community, occupied 80 percent of the quarters at the eastern borders of the Khedive Isma'il's expansions. The 'Abdin quarter is an example of such a predominantly middle-class district.[16]

A new trend began in the 1880s in terms of social classes and economic activities. Al-Azbakiya became a center for private banks, companies, hotels, and brokerage houses, while the Isma'iliya quarter came to be inhabited largely by foreigners. The al-Faggala and al-Zahir quarters began to attract Armenians and Greeks, and the Shubra quarter had a concentration of Egyptian Copts. "In 1897, Shubra's population was 14 percent non-Muslim, while ten years later that number had grown to some 23 percent."[17]

After the 1940s, the top stratum of society in the city's older districts was composed of the middle classes, "while the upper classes moved to Cairo's new European-style districts."[18] For comparison, some types of doorways typical of Cairo's upper-class dwellings are noted in this study, but the majority of doorways presented are those of Egyptian middle-class buildings.

Middle-Class Domestic Architecture in the Nineteenth Century

During the first half of the nineteenth century, Rumi architectural style, introduced by Muhammad 'Ali, who brought engineers, architects, and artisans from Turkey, became dominant in Cairo houses. The palaces constructed for Muhammad 'Ali at al-Qal'a and Shubra were built "in accordance with the new style of one level instead of the older, multi-level style."[19]

The Rumi style was characterized by a plain façade with several projections. The projections were built either from the ground level up, or supported on a 45-degree-angled bracket (plates 2, 7). The brackets in the Rumi style replaced the older Cairene architectural style of using stone corbels (plate 1) as supports. The Rumi style was also characterized by two-story buildings in which the stories contained large, vertical windows (plates 2, 7).[20]

Muhammad 'Ali's sons and heirs, Ibrahim Pasha and 'Abbas Pasha, followed the same building style in their new palaces. Statesmen such as Ahmad Pasha Yakan, Sherif Pasha, and other high-ranking officials played an important role in espousing the Rumi style in Cairo. This style was widely adopted by local people in the older city districts and many examples can still be seen today. The Rumi style is also found, though to a lesser extent, in the new districts of Cairo developed during the reign of Khedive Isma'il. Examples of these include the houses at 26 Shari' 'Abd al-'Aziz, numbers 3 and 5 Shari' 'Ali Pasha Zulfiqar, and 144 Shari' al-Azhar.[21]

Nineteenth-Century Doorways

The design of doorways and other decorative elements was influenced by the architectural style prevailing in the pre-nineteenth century. While Rumi-style architecture became predominant in the closing years of the nineteenth

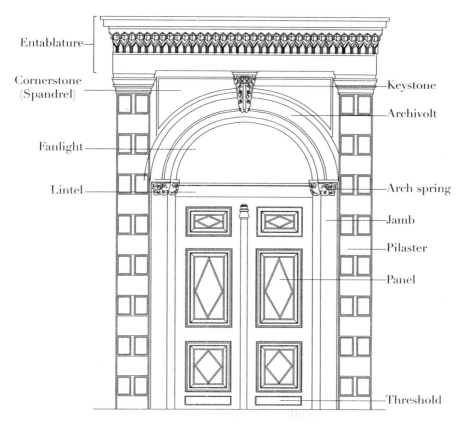

Figure 2: The elements of a late nineteenth-century doorway.

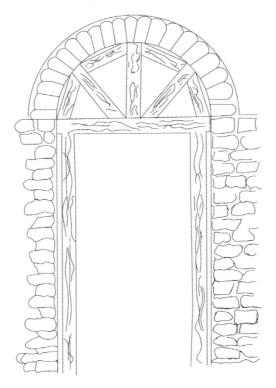

Figure 3: Structure of arched lintel of late nineteenth-century doorways.

century, the Rumi-style doorways of the third quarter of that century differed little from the traditional doorways portrayed by Edward William
Lane in 1836 (figure 1).[22]

The photographs of the late-nineteenth century doorways shown in
this book are set on the same level as the building's façade. The lintel is in
the shape of an arch built of stone or bricks (figure 3).[23] If built of stone,
each voussoir is similar in size and number on each half of the arch, with
the exception of the center voussoir, or keystone, which is longer. The terminals of the arch rest on either side of the wall, constituting the jamb.
Alongside the jamb is the pilaster, the column extending to the height of the

entablature. The area enclosed by the archivolt, entablature, and pilaster is known as the cornerstone or spandrel. The archivolt, cornerstone, entablature, and the building's wall with jamb and pilaster represent the entrance, which together with the door comprise the 'doorway.' Historians and specialists in Islamic architecture have long been amazed by the Islamic decoration of doorways and entrances. "The upper part of the entrance is surrounded by Islamic decorations, which give the doorway a very impressive appearance," noted British orientalist and archaeologist Stanley Lane-Poole in the late nineteenth century.[24]

In the majority of the doorways examined here, the entrances were constructed of stone, a tradition inherited from the Mamluk and Ottoman eras.[25] During the late nineteenth century, "houses were generally two or three stories high and were built of stone from the ground floor."[26] As the doorways were constructed primarily of stone, their decoration was also stone-engraved. Cairene stone-carving artisans were highly skilled in three-dimensional floral and vegetal ornamentation, circular bosses, and abstract motifs (plates 4, 9, 20). Stucco, first used in 1872 in villas, palaces, and buildings in the new districts of Cairo[27] was used for Islamic decorations by Egyptian artisans a few years later in the older quarters of the city. The entrance to 15 Shari' al-Ballasi, dating to AH 1298 / AD 1880, in the Khalifa quarter gives an example of stucco decoration (plate 12).

Decorative Elements of an Entrance

The various parts of an entrance, especially the spandrel, allowed room for a variety of decorative motifs. In the oldest types of entrances, these decorations consisted of geometrical, vegetal, and scriptural ornamentation. A number of decorative styles were applied in the archivolt, such as the zigzag (plate 2), double rows of *muqarnasat* (sing. *muqarnas*) (plates 3, 4, 19, 20), or triple rows of *muqarnasat* (plate 21). Used in Islamic architecture since the Fatimid era,[28] *muqarnasat* were among the most important decorative units used in this type of doorway. The *muqarnasat* take a beehive shape and are arranged in parallel rows one above the other. They are used either as a decorative unit or as a means of gradually altering a decorative shape, as in changing squares to circles in the construction of domes, sometimes serving as supports when placed under a minaret balcony.[29] The archivolt might also be ornamented by a palmette (plate 7), an entrelac (plates 18, 29), or undulating motifs (plate 28).

The arch spring may take the shape of *muqarnasat* (plates 4, 13, 19), a *mima* (a style of parallel and interlocking lines) (plate 21), or circular bosses (plate 9). The arch spring rests on two jambs that form the sides of the entrance. The jamb, which frames the entrance, has no decoration, yet the pilaster takes a variety of forms. The pilaster may end in a crown bearing triglyph ornamentation (plate 2) or taking the shape of plant leaves (plates 7, 10, 27) or double rows of *muqarnasat* (plates 3, 4, 8, 13). The pilaster may be decorated with star-plate ornamentation (plates 18, 21), or circular and semicircular shapes (plates 4, 9). In some instances, the pilaster has no decoration (plates 15, 28).

The most predominant decorative styles of the cornerstone or spandrel are arabesques (figure 4) (plates 7, 15, 18, 20, 28), garlands (plates 10, 14, 22, 23, 26, 27), plant motifs (plates 16, 19), entrelacs (plate 12), fan-shaped designs (plate 2), or circular bosses (plates 8, 9). The spandrel area may be framed by a *jift* and scissors (plate 3) or a *jift* and *mima* motif (plate 21).

The entablature area is usually composed of several cornices or friezes of one or a combination of decorative types. The most common decoration is the *muqarnasat* (plates 3, 6, 8, 13, 19, 21, 28). It may take the shape of an entrelac design (plates 10, 27, 28), the shape of eight-petaled flowers (plates 12, 20), circular bosses (plate 14), or have no decoration (plates 11, 17, 30).

Stone arabesque spandrel with entablature decorated with eight-petaled flowers (plate 20).

Stucco vegetal-decorated spandrel (plate 17).

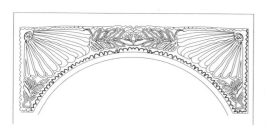

Stone fan-shaped spandrel (plate 2).

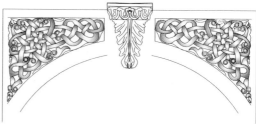

Stucco entrelacs spandrel (plate 12).

Stucco spandrel surrounded by *jifi* and scissors motifs with keystone decorated with three rows of *muqarnasat* (plate 3).

Stucco garland spandrel (plate 10).

Figure 4: Cornerstones (spandrels) from nineteenth-century doorways.

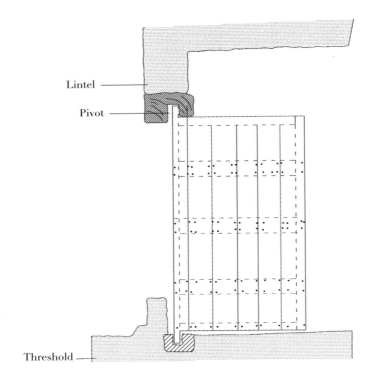

Figure 5: Design of one-leaf doors of the nineteenth century.

Structure and Design of Doors

With the introduction of Rumi architectural styles at the beginning of the nineteenth century during the reign of Muhammad 'Ali, double-leaf doors predominated in Cairo buildings. Formerly, entrances consisted of single doors,[30] as found in the building at 8 Harat Birguwan (plate 2), one of the oldest doorways photographed in this book. One-leaf doors were fixed and moved by two wooden rods extending from either side of the door's stile (figure 5).[31] The upper extension hinged on a pivot fixed to the lintel,[32] while the lower extension is fixed to another pivot in the threshold, which serves to carry the door's weight (plates 2, 14).

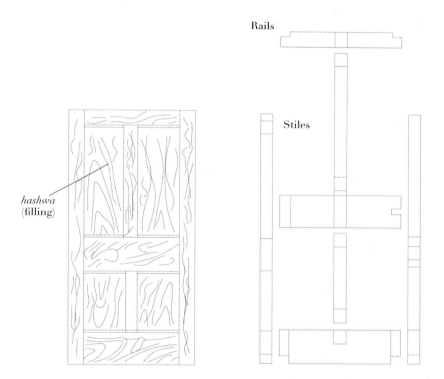

Figure 6: Structure of late nineteenth- and early twentieth-century doors.

During the reign of Muhammad 'Ali the construction of doors moved away from the older *gama'iya* method, where doors were assembled by joining comb-shaped wood pieces without the use of adhesives or nails, in favor of simpler methods using stiles, rails, and filling enclosures *(hashawat)*.[33] In the new method each leaf of the door consisted of longitudinal stiles and cross-piece rail frames fixed with dovetailing joints (figure 6).[34] In this method, there are two stiles connected by several rails, two in the upper and lower part and one or more in the center. The stiles and rails method used in the construction of doors is similar to the method used in the construction of double-leaf doors in Fatimid mosques (such as the doors of al-Fakahani Mosque on Shari' al-Mu'izz). These types of doors contain horizontal and vertical *hashawat* of wood-engraved decoration, a method ignored later during the Mamluk and Ottoman periods when the *hashawat* were made from comb-shaped wood pieces connected in the *gama'iya* method.

From the outside, and depending upon the number of rails present in each leaf, the door is divided into sections or panels. In two-panel doors the upper panel is the largest (plates 4, 18, 21), while in three-panel doors the center panel is the largest (plates 11, 28). In four-panel doors the third panel from the top is the largest (plate 7). These panels may have arabesque motifs (plate 18) or square, fan, or rhomboid shapes (plates 7, 11, 28). Some simple panels have no decorative figures (plates 6).

Early nineteenth-century doors (as shown in figure 1) do not include fanlights, a tradition that can be traced in some doors until the late twentieth century (plates 2, 7). Fanlights were added to doors by the late nineteenth century and gradually became one of the components of doors, as seen in the oldest door pictured in this book (dated 1872, plate 25). The wrought-iron fanlight takes a semicircle shape. At the center of the straight edge is a small, semicircular section representing the hub, where the date of the building's construction is usually inscribed. The fanlight's wrought iron reflects a variety of decorative motifs characteristic of nineteenth-century style doors (figure 7).

Middle-Class Domestic Architecture in the Twentieth Century

The second half of the nineteenth century witnessed the introduction of the European neoclassical and neo-Baroque styles (generally referred to as the 'European styles'). These styles were "rich in stucco façade decoration."[35] During the reign of Khedive Isma'il "European architects were encouraged

Fanlight of large decorated plate in the middle surrounded by semicircular motifs (plate 9).

Fanlight of one central circular unit and two larger semicircular units having an unusual two hubs inscribed with the date of the building's construction: AH 1306 / AD 1888 (Midan Sidi 'Abd al-Gawad, Bulaq).

Fanlight of nine spokes ending with arrowheads with the hub containing the date of the building (AH 1291 / AD 1874) (plate 8).

Fanlight of radiating spokes topped with arrowheads and crescents with stars (plate 21).

Fanlight of circular, semicircular, and pear-shaped motifs (plate 13).

Figure 7: Fanlights from nineteenth-century doorways.

to come and practice their profession in Cairo. Most of these architects were Italian (e.g., Mario Rossi), French (e.g., Alexander Marcel), or British (e.g., Edwin Erlanger)."[36] The European style flourished, marking the character of the new districts of Cairo founded by Khedive Isma'il.

An increasing number of immigrants to Egypt during the second half of the nineteenth century, notably after the British occupation in 1882, played an important role in spreading the European style. The population of Cairo in 1882 was approximately 374,800, including 22,420 foreign residents (7,000 Turks; 5,000 French; 3,400 Italians; 1,800 Austrians; 1,000 British; and 450 Germans).[37] By 1907, the number of foreign residents in Egypt had reached 151,400, of whom 76,170 lived in Cairo and were concentrated in the newer districts.[38]

Foreigners brought with them various architectural styles and traditions. In the houses they constructed, each floor was similar in layout while each room had a definite function, such as bedroom, reception room, living room, kitchen, and private bathroom. The older, traditional architectural style designed each floor differently and assigned a variety of functions to each room.[39]

Twentieth-century, middle-class Cairene architecture was the product of both European and Egyptian influences. European architects in Cairo from the third quarter of the nineteenth century "were quite familiar with the ideas of continuity and revival in architecture. They applied comparable concepts of reintroducing traditional architecture in Cairo, developing what might be called the neo-Islamic style."[40] Nationalism also contributed to the development of this neo-Islamic style. "The idea of nationalism existed as early as the British occupation in 1882 but lay dormant until becoming a national movement in the 1919 Revolution. This revolution aimed at giving practical expression to the national spirit, of which architecture was one aspect."[41]

Another factor in the development of the revival elements in neo-Islamic style was the return of Egyptians sent on training missions to Europe. Scholarships to study in Europe were an important source of educated and well-trained Egyptian architects. Of forty-four architects on mission between 1908 and 1931, twenty-eight were sent to Paris and Liverpool. After their return to Egypt, they became the nuclei of the new architectural schools. Some of them worked in the wake of the Islamic revival style, hoping to develop a national style.[42] In the same spirit, the School of Fine Arts opened in 1930, providing a new source of architects and decorators.[43]

Some art historians have suggested that the revival of Islamic decorative styles in what became known as neo-Islamic style was a direct result of "the spread of stucco workshops and the new stucco technique introduced by foreign builders."[44] They claim that the stucco technique, which has been used in the decoration of mosques since the pre-Fatimid period[45] (plate 88), greatly facilitated the execution of complex Islamic motifs and has been used by local builders in doorway decoration for a long time.

The trend toward building in the spirit of Islamic traditional styles can be seen notably in the newer districts of Cairo, both in public and residential buildings. The renowned architect Mustafa Pasha Fahmi is credited with the design of the Egyptian Engineers Society (1930) and the Doctors Syndicate (1941). The neo-Islamic trend can also be seen in buildings such as the head offices of Bank Misr in Cairo (1927) and Alexandria (1929).

Neo-Islamic style was further modified by some Egyptian architects who synthesized it with the neo-pharaonic style. "They found this a more convincing style for Muslims and Copts, thereby expressing the principle idea of the 1919 Revolution. The mausoleum of Sa'd Zaghlul (1928) built by Mustafa Fahmi is an example of this trend."[46]

The architecture of the old districts of Cairo during the twentieth century was greatly influenced by that of the new districts. Old Cairo "witnessed a gradual decline of traditional architecture and a break in its evolution."[47] One of the negative effects of this trend was the collapse of the associations and guilds working in the fields of construction and decoration. Trade guilds had declined under pressure from growing state power during the reign of Muhammad 'Ali and his successors as the state became the largest employer in the construction sector, resulting in the creation of new industries and the establishment of new training institutions such as schools and factories, as well as the extension of the state's building activities to cities other than Cairo and Alexandria.

According to the census of 1883 there were 198 craftsman guilds in Cairo, with 63,480 members. Among these were 262 sawyers, 1,615 carpenters, 98 wood engravers, and 15 inlayers of ivory and shell.[48] In 1888, "the government forbade guild leaders from collecting taxes imposed on crafts and in 1890 it issued a law giving freedom to individuals to practice any craft, thereby canceling mandatory guild apprenticeships."[49] Such legislation spelled the gradual demise of many guilds involved in construction and decoration. The disappearance of woodcarvers and carpenters as well as builders who constructed and decorated doorways led to a decline in the use of local and Islamic decoration in the construction of doorways. Districts in Cairo are named after such crafts and trade groups that have since disappeared, such as Harat al-Khashabin (woodworkers), al-Fahamin (charcoal makers), al-Nahasin (coppersmiths), al-Siyufiya (swordsmiths), and al-Qirabiya (water-skin tanners).

While the neo-Islamic, eclectic, and European styles proliferated in new Cairo and were echoed in old Cairo, in old Cairo the local Egyptian *mu'allim*s (master craftsmen) rather than the academically trained architects remained responsible for building construction. They kept architectural and decorative traditions alive through oral transmission and apprentice-ship of younger generations. They continued to emulate the secular and religious architecture around them in old Cairo.

Although the trends discussed contributed to the destruction of significant portions of the old Cairo districts and their architecture, the Cairene *mu'allim*s continued to develop their own styles. In façades with large areas of wooden bays they added new elements such as window screens with horizontal slats. Woodworked façades were still rich in Islamic decoration, especially abstract motifs. Their architectural style reflected a combination of traditional *mashrabiya* and windows of northern Mediter-ranean origin. Woodworking elements might be in the same plane as the façade (plate 82) or applied to projecting units distributed vertically and hor-izontally on the façade. One can find four woodwork projections, either open (plate 83) or closed (plate 84), as well as double woodwork projections, either open or closed (plates 85, 86). In the first decade of the twentieth century this style of architectural woodwork flourished in many districts of old Cairo.

Twentieth-Century Doorways

The revival of neo-Islamic architecture at the beginning of the twentieth century had a huge impact on the structure and design of doorways of the period. Some doorways were set in the same plane as the façade, while oth-ers were recessed, imitating Ottoman secular and religious tradition, where doorways were set back at some depth from the façade, allowing the accom-modation of two outdoor stone benches *(mastaba* or *maksala)* facing one another (plates 45, 46). The doorway took the shape of an arch, which had the function of distributing the weight of the wall above it onto columns.[50]

In doorways that are in the same level of the façade, the lintel may be straight (figure 9)[51] or curved (figure 10)[52] and constructed of either stone or brick. Some doorways of this period keep the old partitions of the upper part

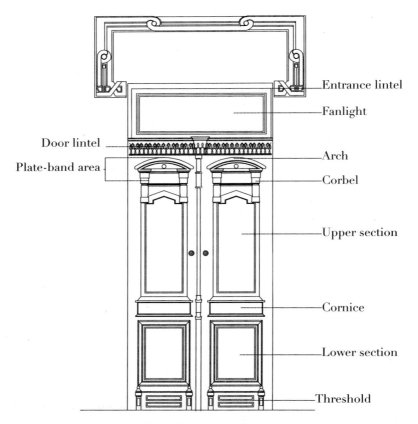

Figure 8: The elements of a late twentieth-century doorway.

of the entrance—the entablature, spandrel, and archivolt (plates 36, 37)—but in others these partitions are neglected. Through the 1930s and 1940s, these partitions disappeared completely, replaced in some cases by European-style pediments (plates 68, 69, 70). As an architectural unit, the keystones of the doorways of the twentieth century maintained their decorative function. The keystone reflects the artisan's decorative capabilities, in turn expressing a cultural and artistic background (plates 55, 61, 87). In some cases it also indicates the house owner's religious faith (plate 76).

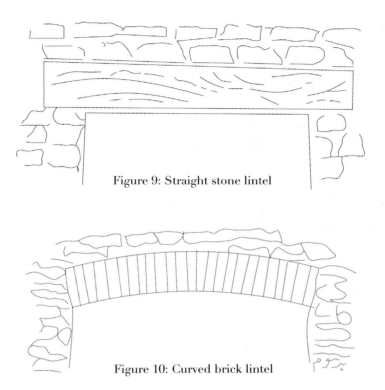

Figure 9: Straight stone lintel

Figure 10: Curved brick lintel

The double doors of the twentieth century moved on hinges fixed to the jamb. In these types of doors, it became customary to use a *sama'* or knocker for visitors to announce their presence. The iron *sama'* was in the shape of a handle attached to the mid-upper section of the door. Nineteenth-century doors did not have a knocker.[53]

The leaves of the doors of this period, instead of being made only from various kinds of wood as during the nineteenth century (plates 33, 34, 35, 38), were made of wrought iron and wood, especially the upper sections. This technique soon prevailed, spreading in both the old and new districts of Cairo and in dwellings irrespective of social class. The use of wrought iron in the construction of double doors in Cairo's middle-class houses dates back to at least 1906, as seen in the house at 5 Harat al-Qirabiya, Shari' al-Mu'izz (plate 47). Wrought iron was used primarily as a decorative tool in the fan-light and upper section of a door. Later on, some doors were constructed entirely of iron (plates 41, 43, 44). Iron doors were made for the khedivial buildings in Shari' 'Imad al-Din (1911) and the style rapidly spread to other Cairo districts. Apart from its decorative function, the use of wrought iron in the upper sections of doors played a special role in the expression of nationalism and the revival of Islamic architecture in Cairo's old districts.

From the 1910s onward, two decorative motifs predominated in the upper section of doors: the serpent and the crescent. The use of a serpent as a symbol in doors dates to a pharaonic tradition, reflecting the belief in a serpent's magic powers of protection, especially at temple entrances. A symbol of immortality, the serpent is also found in the pharaonic crown, bracelets, necklaces, and earrings. The crescent is an Islamic symbol reflecting the designer's religious beliefs. The combination of the two symbols side by side on a door reflected the unity of the two elements of the nation, Copts and Muslims, a theme of the nationalist movement at the time. The pharaonic serpent and Muslim crescent also suggest an artistic interaction between motion and stability.

Structure and Design of Early Twentieth-Century Doors

The door leaf is divided into five different parts—the upper section, lower section, plate-band, cornice, and threshold—of which the largest, the upper section, represents about half the height of the door. Above this is the top section, called the plate-band, and a raised wood molding, the cornice, separating the upper and lower sections. The width of the cornice is usually the same as that of the upper and lower sections (plates 45, 46, 53) and sometimes it is slightly wider (plates 47, 48, 49). In most cases the door handle is affixed to the cornice. Below the lower section is the raised wood molding known as the door's threshold, which may extend to the lower edge of the door. The threshold has several decorative shapes (plates 47, 48, 49, 51, 52). Above the door leaf is the fanlight.

The Upper Section

Irrespective of its length compared to the total length of the leaf, the upper section (figure 11) has various forms, such as the *mihrab* (plates 45, 46, 48, 53) or rectangle (plates 47, 54, 55, 56). The upper part of this section generally takes the shape of a narrow or wide semicircle (plates 50, 58, 57, 60).

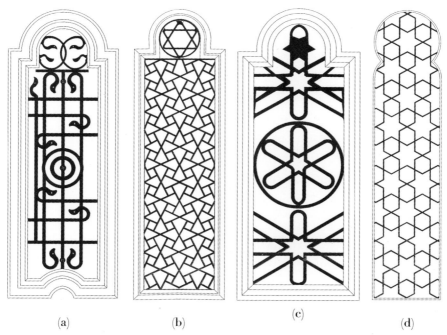

(a) (b) (c) (d)

(a) Snake heads of different sizes and directions (plate 60).

(b) Four-sided geometrical motifs of different shapes (plate 50).

(c) Six- and eight-pointed stars with arms (plate 52).

(d) Six-sided shapes with six-pointed stars (plate 46).

Figure 11: Wrought iron from the upper section *(shura'a)* of twentieth-century double doorways.

Introduction

Egyptian blacksmiths used the image of a snake in s-shaped designs. They used lengths of iron strips representing the snake's whole body with the head and tail curved in different directions (plates 56, 57, 58). In other cases they used the snake's head or tail. Beautiful examples are found of a snake head in the form of circles or semicircles interlocking or opposing each other (plates 59, 60) and an impressive example of a snake tail motif (plate 64).

Apart from snake motifs, hexagonal flower shapes were affixed in the center of the crescent (plates 55, 58). One or two flower ornaments may also be distributed throughout the panel (plates 54, 55, 59). Other Islamic decorations were used such as geometrical abstract motifs of four-sided (plates 49, 50) and six-sided (plate 46) shapes of various sizes.

Plate-band Area

The area extends from the edge of the upper section to the top of the door and includes decorative elements usually encompassing two corbels. Frequently, above the ornamentation and corbels is an arch. The decorations may be in the form of two or three rows of *muqarnasat* (plates 48, 50) with or without corbels. The plate-band may also take human, animal, or plant forms (plates 54, 57, 68, 76), plant motifs inside a wide triangle (plates 59, 66), or three pyramidal shapes enclosed by corbels (plates 60, 73). In some cases this area is free of decoration (plate 58).

The Lower Section

In doors made entirely of wood, or wood and wrought iron, the lower section generally takes a square shape. This lower section is composed of one panel (plates 45) consisting of two (plates 60, 61), three (plate 78), or four (plate 73) parts. In some examples, the lower section is rectangular (plates 49, 50, 51, 75). Islamic decorations such as a star-plate (plates 39, 42, 45,

47, 48, 51), the *mufruka* (plate 52), *ma'kali* (plate 49), or plant forms (plates 54, 56, 62, 68, 75) often decorate the lower section.

The star-plate consists of a shield *(al-tirs)* in the center surrounded by several polygonal pieces *(kinda)* that may be eight (figure 12, plate 47), ten (plate 39, upper section), twelve, or sixteen in number. The *ma'kali* unit consists of rectangular insets *(hashawat)* arranged vertically and horizontally, encompassing square pieces of *hashawat* in between. The *ma'kali* ornamentation might appear in a straight or an oblique position (figure 13, plate 49). The *mufruka* unit is an artistic representation of the magnificent word of Allah in Arabic script (figure 14, plate 52). In other instances, this lower section shows a motif representing the sun disk with rays (plates 64, 65), a form echoing the central religious symbolism of the pharaoh Akhenaten (also known as Amenhotep IV, 1375–1358 BC).

Figure 12: Star-plate

Figure 13: *Ma'kali*

Figure 14: *Mufruka*

Fanlight

At the beginning of the twentieth century the shape of a fanlight changed from a semicircle to a rectangle in order to conform to the door's architecture. The fanlight usually contained the same decorative motifs used in the door's upper section. In this style of doorway, we find some decorative elements in the area above the fanlight, such as projecting (plate 50) or joggled (plate 65) voussoirs. This area is sometimes encircled by decorations in the form of *jift* and *mima* motifs (plate 49). In other cases the area above the fanlight contains a pediment in Greco-Roman (plates 68, 69) or art nouveau (plate 70) style.

Dating of Nineteenth- and Twentieth-Century Doorways

In determining or estimating the date of a nineteenth-century doorway, three record sources are required: the public tax record from the Dar al-Mahfuzat bi-l-Qal'a, the construction date (if present) inscribed on the fanlight's hub, and the building's architectural style.

The public tax records were organized in eight-year periods, and records are available for the years 1902–1909, 1910–1917, 1918–1925, etc. Unfortunately, the extant records do not include entries prior to the period 1902–1909. In a few cases the records of 1902–1909 mention some buildings founded a year or two prior to 1902, apparently to determine the exact year of construction in estimating tax value. The houses photographed in plates 16 and 17 are mentioned in the records as being constructed in 1900 and 1899 respectively, and their owners are recorded.

In some instances the date of the building is known from the date of its construction inscribed on the fanlight hub. This tradition prevailed particularly in the Bulaq district. One of these examples is the oldest doorway included in this study, the house at 25 Darb al-Kalafta in Bulaq dating to AH 1289 / AD 1872. In cases where early doorways are dated, the only tax records available are from the period 1910–1917, and the owners listed could be the heirs of the original builder.

Construction dates inscribed on fanlight hubs are of great help in determining the date of a doorway, especially if the original doors have been replaced by newer ones. For example, the original doorway of 29 Darb al-Habala, Midan Sayyida 'Aysha, dated AH 1292 / AD 1875 in the hub of its fanlight, has been replaced by a new twentieth-century-style door.

The architectural style of a building is also helpful in determining the date of a doorway. The door in plate 30 is from the twentieth century, but it seems clear from the fanlight, with nine spokes of iron ending in crescents and arrowheads, and the building's style (as in the first-story windows) that the original nineteenth-century door was replaced.

In the absence of public tax records one must compare the known history of one doorway to deduce the unknown date of other doorways in the same street or alley. For example, the house at 15 Shari' Ballasi in the al-Khalifa quarter (plate 12) dates from AH 1298 / AD 1880 as inscribed on the fanlight hub. It may be assumed with some confidence that the three houses adjacent to this house on the same street are of the same period.

Identification of twentieth-century doorways is easier since the public tax records (if available) generally state the exact date of construction. To date a doorway, one depends upon a combination of information from the tax records and the date of construction written on the keystone (plate 39) or the upper section of the door leaf (plate 52).

Studies of architectural and decorative elements found in Cairo's late nineteenth- and early twentieth-century buildings deal primary with the Cairo of Khedive Isma'il. This book focuses on the doorways of middle-class houses built in Cairo's old neighborhoods during this period. During the first half of the nineteenth century, Rumi architectural style, introduced by Muhammad 'Ali, was adopted widely by locals in the older city districts. The design, structure, and decorative elements of the doorways are greatly influenced by the prevailing architectural style. The Rumi-style doorways of the third quarter of the nineteenth century differed little from the traditional doorways predominant in old Cairo, reflecting some features of pre–nineteenth-century doorways.

Doorways of the late nineteenth century are set on the same level as the building's façade. The lintel is in the form of a stone or bricks arch. The terminals of the arch rest on either side of the wall, constituting the jamb. Alongside the jamb is the pilaster, the column extended to the level of the entablature. The section between the archivolt, the entablature, and the pilaster is known as the cornerstone or spandrel. The previous sections, which represent the entrance, together with the door itself, comprise the doorway. The entrance, especially the upper section, in particular the spandrel, exhibit a variety of decorative motifs which give the Cairo doorways of the nineteenth century their impressive appearance. Traditional early nineteenth-century doors are of one leaf made of wood assembled in the *gama'iya* method. Under the influence of Rumi-style architecture the doors became two-leafs constructed by the simpler method of stiles and rails enclosing fillings *(hashawat)*. One-leaf doors moved and were fixed by hinging on two pivots present in the lintel and threshold of the entrance. Doorways of the early twentieth century consist of double leafs, moved on hinges fixed to the jamb. The usual section of the upper parts of the entrance gradually disappeared, replaced by Greco-Roman or art nouveau style pediments.

The doors of this period were not only made from various kinds of wood, but of wrought iron and wood, and sometimes completely of iron. As the design and decorative characters of the doorway are directly influenced by the architectural style of the building, that style is greatly influenced by prevailing social, economic, and political factors. The wrought iron used in the decoration of the upper section and fanlight acted as a means by which both the middle-class owners and blacksmiths of old Cairo reflected their political loyalties. Early twentieth-century doors are characterized mainly by serpent and crescent motifs. Widely present in doorways in Cairo's old districts, these two decorative units are considered a direct reflection of the nationalist movement that inspired the 1919 Revolution.

Notes

1. Richard C. Foltz, *Islam and Ecology: A Bestowed Trust* (Cambridge: Harvard University Press, 2003), p. 364.

2. Ibn al-Hagg al-Fasi, *al-Madkhal* (Cairo: al-Maktabat al-Tijari al-Kubra, 1929), p. 70.

3. Ibid., p. 195.

4. Nelly Hanna, *Buyut al-Qahira fi-l-qarnayn al-sabi' 'ashar wa-l-thamin 'ashar: dirasa ijtima'iya mi'mariya*, trans. Halim Tuson (Cairo: al-'Arabi li-l-Nashr wa-l-Tawzi', 1993), p. 221.

5. Ibid., p. 238.

6. Ibid., pp. 240–41.

7. Ibid., p. 165.

8. Egyptian Public Tax Record: 1910–1917, file no. 10174/205/32, p. 8.

9. Egyptian Public Tax Record: 1902–1909, file no. 9696/195/32, p. 166.

10. Egyptian Public Tax Record: 1902–1909, file no. 10174/205/32, p. 7.

11. Egyptian Public Tax Record: 1902–1909, file no. 12432/258/32, p. 192.

12. Egyptian Public Tax Record: 1910–1917, file no. 5748/107/32, p. 42.

13. Egyptian Public Tax Record: 1910–1917, file no. 10315/208/32, p. 2.

14. Jean-Luc Arnaud, *al-Qahira: iqamat madina haditha (1867–1907)*, trans. Halim Tuson (Cairo: al-Majlis al-A'la li-l-Thaqafa, 2002), p. 222.

15. Ibid., p. 229.

16. Ibid., p. 266.

17. Ibid., p. 276.

18. Mohamed Scharabi, *Stadt und Architectur im Zeitalter des europäschen Kolonial-ismus* (Tübingen: Verlag Ernst Wasmuth, 1989), p. 145.

19. 'Ali Mubarak, *al-Khitat al-tawfiqiya* (Cairo: Dar al-Kutub al-Misriya, 1969), p. 216.

20. Nihal S. Tamraz, *Nineteenth-Century Cairene Houses and Palaces* (Cairo: The American University in Cairo Press, 1998), p. 24.

21. Ibid., p. 26.

22. Edward William Lane, *al-Misriyun al-muhdithun, sham'ilahum wa 'adatihim*, trans. Adli Tahir Nur (Cairo: Dar al-Nashr li-l-Gami'at al-Misriya, 1975), p. 14.

23. Muhammad Wasfi, *al-Qawa'id al-asasiya fi-l-'imara al-misriya* (Cairo: Matba'at Madrasat al-Funun wa-l-Sana'i' al-Khidiwiya, 1901), p. 42.

24. Stanley Lane-Poole, *Sirit al-Qahira*, trans. Hasan Ibrahim (Cairo: al-Nahda al-Misriya, 1950), p. 30.

25. Tamraz, *Nineteenth-Century Cairene Houses and Palaces*, p. 36.

26. Stanley Lane-Poole, *The Art of the Saracens in Egypt* (London: Chapman and Hall, 1998), p. 75.

27. Tamraz, *Nineteenth-Century Cairene Houses and Palaces*, p. 36.

28. Ahmad Fikry, *Masajid wa madaris al-Qahira* (Cairo: Dar al-Ma'arif, 1965), p. 205.

29. 'Assim Muhammad Rizk, *Dirasat fi-l-fann al-islami* (Cairo: Supreme Council of Antiquities, 1995), p. 150.

30. Clot Bey, *Lamha 'amma ila Misr*, part I, trans. Muhammad Mas'ud (Cairo: Matba'at Abu al-Hul, 1981), p. 391.

31. Nessim Henry, *Mari Girgis: Village de Haute-Egypte* (Cairo: Institut Français d'Archéologie Orientale, 1988), p. 45.

32. Lane-Poole, *The Art of the Saracens in Egypt*, p. 76.

33. Mubarak, *al-Khitat al-tawfiqiya*, p. 216.

34. 'Abd al-Halim Muhammad, *al-Akhshab wa-l-nigara wa-l-naggar* (Cairo: Matba'at al-Samah, 1928), p. 65.

35. Tamraz, *Nineteenth-Century Cairene Houses and Palaces*, pp. 18, 36.

36. Tarek M. Sakr, *Early Twentieth-Century Islamic Architecture in Cairo* (Cairo: The American University in Cairo Press, 1992), p. 12.

37. Mubarak, *al-Khitat al-tawfiqiya*, p. 244.

38. André Raymond, *al-Qahira: tarikh hadira*, trans. Latif Farag (Cairo: Dar al-Fikr li-l-Dirasat wa-l-Nashr wa-l-Tawzi', 1993), p. 231.

39. Mubarak, *al-Khitat al-tawfiqiya*, p. 216.

40. Sakr, *Early Twentieth Century Islamic Architecture in Cairo*, p. 13.

41. Ibid., p. 12.

42. Ibid., p. 14.

43. Ibid.

44. Tamraz, *Nineteenth-Century Cairene Houses and Palaces*, p. 39.

45. Fikry, *Masajid wa madaris al-Qahira*, p. 174.

46. Sakr, *Early Twentieth Century Islamic Architecture in Cairo*, p. 16.

47. Ibid., p. 8.

48. Mubarak, *al-Khitat al-tawfiqiya*, p. 248.

49. G. Pier, *Dirasat fi-l-tarikh al-ijtima'i li-Misr al-haditha*, trans. 'Abd al-Khaliq Lashin (Cairo: Maktabat al-Hurriya al-Haditha, 1976), p. 311.

50. Rizk, *Dirasat fi-l-fann al-islami*, p. 149.

51. Wasfi, *al-Qawa'id al-asasiya fi-l-'imara al-misriya*, p. 42.

52. Ibid.

53. Lane-Poole, *Sirat al-Qahira*, p. 30.

THE PLATES

PLATE 1

▲ 25 Darb al-Kazazzin, Shari'
Bab al-Wazir. This house
dates to the early nineteenth
century. Note the stone corbels, characteristic of
pre–nineteenth-century
buildings, which carry the
projection of the first story.
The property was owned by
al-Sayyid 'Ali Shalabi al-
Harriri.

▲ The entablature comprises friezes, the lower being the largest
and containing five six-petaled flowers surrounded by six
groups of double-leaf motifs. This is not the original door.

PLATE 2

▲ This is a one-leaf doorway with a zigzag archivolt. The spandrel has a fan-shaped decoration. Between the two spandrels are plant motifs in the form of ten leaves facing one another. Above these plant motifs is a small opening in the shape of a *mihrab*. The pilaster crown has a triglyph decoration.

▼ 8 Shari' Birguwan, al-Gamaliya. Dated to the mid-nineteenth century, this house was owned by the *waqf ahli* of Abu al-Ma'ali al-Gohary. Note the 45-degree-angled bracket and large, vertical windows typical of Rumi architecture.

PLATE 3

▲ 2 'Atfat al-Ashkar, Shari'
al-Bayumi, al-Husayniya.
Dated to the third quarter
of the nineteenth century, it
was the property of the
heirs of 'Ali Effendi Yusuf.

▲ The archivolt, keystone, pilaster crown, and entablature
are decorated with a double row of *muqarnasat*. The
spandrel has no decoration but is surrounded by a *jift* and
scissors motif.

PLATE 4

▲ 12 Shari' al-Hud, off Shari' al-Bayumi, al-
Husayniya. Dated to the third quarter of the
nineteenth century, this building belonged
to the heirs of 'Abd al-Karim Zaydan.

▶ Detail of the upper section of the doorway showing the archivolt, arch spring,
and entablature with *muqarnasat* decoration. Note the cornerstone and
pilaster of projecting circular bosses.

► This is an impressive stone entrance. The archivolt consists of a double row of *muqarnasat*, as does the entablature and arch spring. The pilaster is distinguished by two decorative circular units: the first consists of trifolded leaves arranged in four groups and the second is a leaf motif arranged in four groups. The spandrel has three decorative units similar to the decorative unit of the pilaster but in two different sizes, the large one located between the two smaller ones.

PLATE 5

▼ 69 Shari' al-Sawabi, off Shari' al-Bayumi. This house is dated to the late nineteenth century and was the property of al-Shaykh 'Abd al-Karim Bayumi.

▲ The double-leaf doorway consists of two panels. The entablature comprises two rows of *muqarnasat* and the spandrel is without decoration.

PLATE 6

▲ 11 Khukhat al-Karamani, Shari' al-Bayumi. Dated to the late nineteenth century, this property was owned by al-Sayyid Nagi 'Abd al-Nasr.

▲ The entablature of the doorway is distinguished by separate units of *muqarnasat*. The spandrel is without decoration.

PLATE 7

▼ 55 Shari' Bab al-Wazir.
Dated to the third quarter
of the nineteenth century,
it belonged to the heirs of
Isma'il Pasha Siddiq and
Muhammad Bey Tawfiq.

▲ A Rumi-style doorway with a double-leaf door. Each
leaf has four panels having a different geometrical
shape. The archivolt consists of palm fronds and the
spandrel consists of a lovely arabesque decoration.
The pilaster has two friezes of entrelac motifs.

PLATE 8

▲ 18 Sikkat al-Mahgar, al-Qal'a, was the property of the heirs of Hassan Effendi Kamil.

▲ The voussoirs of the archivolt take the form of *muqarnasat*. The pilaster crown is decorated with three rows of *muqarnasat*. The entablature consists of two friezes; the lower is in the form of one row of *muqarnasat*. The spandrels have projecting bosses and the fanlight consists of nine spokes ending in spears. The date on the door's fanlight is AH 1291 (AD 1874).

PLATE 9

▼ 9 Shariʻ al-Ballasi, off Shariʻ al-Ashraf, al-Khalifa, dates to the third quarter of the nineteenth century.

▲ Bosses are a dominant decorative motif in this impressive entrance. The artisan uses *jift* and *mima* designs to frame the parts of the entrance and uses them to create circular bosses in various sizes. Two bosses are arranged on either side of the arch spring. One large boss at the top of the archivolt separates the two spandrels, each containing its own boss. The archivolt and entablature have entrelac ornamentation.

PLATE 10

▲ 6 Shari' al-Ballasi, off Shari' al-Ashraf, al-Khalifa. The building is dated to the third quarter of the nineteenth century and was owned by Ahmad Mahgub.

▲ The spandrel has a garland motif. The entablature consists of two friezes, the lower with entrelac decoration being wider.

PLATE 11

14 Shariʿ al-Ballasi, off Shariʿ al-Ashraf, al-Khalifa. This property belonged to the heirs of Hassan al-Qamah and is dated to the third quarter of the nineteenth century. The original double-leaf doorway has three differently shaped panels. The voussoirs of the archivolt take the form of *muqarnasat* framed by a *jift* and *mima* motif. The spandrel is distinguished by a six-pointed star in the center of the entrelac decoration.

▶ Detail from the upper section of the doorway showing the fanlight with a large circular unit in the center containing a six-petaled flower.

PLATE 12

▲ 15 Shari' al-Ballasi, off Shari' al-
Ashraf, al-Khalifa. The house was
the property of 'Ali al-Numrusi
and Taha Ahmad al-Naggar.

▲ The distinctive spandrel has magnificent stucco entrelac
motifs. The entablature is distinguished by a broad cornice of eight-petaled flowers surrounded by arcs. In the
hub of the fanlight is the date, AH 1298 (AD 1880).

PLATE 13

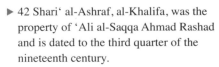

◄ The double-leaf doorway consists of three panels. The archivolt has leaf motifs, while the entablature, arch spring, and the pilaster crown are decorated with a double row of *muqarnasat*. The fanlight is characteristic of the period.

► 42 Shari' al-Ashraf, al-Khalifa, was the property of 'Ali al-Saqqa Ahmad Rashad and is dated to the third quarter of the nineteenth century.

PLATE 18

▲ 17 Darb Nasr, Shari'
Bulaq al-Gadid. This
Rumi-style house dated to
the third quarter of the
nineteenth century was
owned by Sufya Hanim
Huzu, widow of al-
Khawaga Henry.

▲ The Rumi-style doorway has double leaves, each with three panels,
of which the middle panel is largest. The middle and lower panels
have arabesque ornamentation with a hub inside an elliptical frame.
The archivolt has entrelac motifs. The arabesque ornamentation of
the spandrel is surrounded by a *jift* and *mima* motif. The pilaster
has a star-shaped pattern, visible in the upper portion.

PLATE 19

◀ *Muqarnasat* motifs decorate various elements of the entrance to this one-leaf doorway: the archivolt, the arch spring, the entablature, and the pilaster crown. The spandrel is adorned with a branch and leaves.

▶ 7 Shari' al-Khusus, off Shari' Bulaq al-Gadid, dates to the third quarter of the nineteenth century.

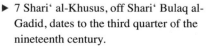

PLATE 20

▲ 35 Harat al-Nuqali, Shari' al-
Shaykh Farrag, Bulaq. Dated to
the third quarter of the nineteenth century, this property was
owned by Muhammad Ahmad
al-Zayat.

▲ The archivolt consists of two rows of *muqarnasat*
and the entablature of eight-petaled flowers surrounded by arcs, a motif that extends along the
ground floor façade. The spandrel's arabesque
ornamentations are unique. The pilaster has hol-
lowed decorative reliefs.

PLATE 21

This Rumi-style doorway features *jift* and *mima* motifs and a triple row of *muqarnasat* enclosing an ornate fanlight of wrought iron inscribed with the date of construction, AH 1295 (AD 1878). The fanlight's radiating spokes are topped with alternating arrowheads and crescent and star designs. The spandrel has arabesque decoration and the pilasters are ornamented with star-plates.

▶ 1 Shari' Rab'a al-Ruz, Suq al-'Asr, Bulaq. The property was owned by the heirs of Hassan al-Kafrawi. It has since been demolished.

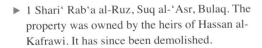

PLATE 22

▲ 33 Darb al-Shaykh Bidayr,
Midan Sidi 'Abd al-Gawad,
Bulaq. Dated to the third
quarter of the nineteenth
century, this house was
owned by Hassan Hifta
and Maryam bint Himayda.

▲ Double-leaf doorway of three panels; the upper is the
largest. The archivolt contains geometrical abstracts
and plant motifs. Splendid garland ornamentation decorates the spandrel. The unique fanlight has seven
inverted arrowheads.

PLATE 23

◀ Garland ornamentation adorns the spandrel of this one-leaf doorway. The entablature has two bosses. Trilobed-leaf motifs arranged in fours decorate the pilaster.

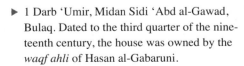

▶ 1 Darb 'Umir, Midan Sidi 'Abd al-Gawad, Bulaq. Dated to the third quarter of the nineteenth century, the house was owned by the *waqf ahli* of Hasan al-Gabaruni.

PLATE 24

▲ The fanlight, showing ornate wrought-iron decorations with the construction date inscribed in the hub, AH 1294 (AD 1877).

▲ 14 Darb al-Galladin, Midan Sidi 'Abd al-Gawad, Bulaq. Dated AH 1294 (AD 1877), this house was owned by al-Mu'allim Muhammad al-Haddad. The upper part of the entrance is without the usual sectional elements and is devoid of decoration.

PLATE 25

2 Darb al-Qalafta, Midan Sidi
'Abd al-Gawad, Bulaq, dated
AH 1289 (AD 1872), was
owned by Rabi' al-Siba'i.

The fanlight with its five long
arrows and six short spokes
and the date of construction,
AH 1289 (AD 1872), inscribed
in the hub.

▶ The lower section of this double-leaf doorway is the only original part of the door that remains. Nine projecting voussoirs shape the archivolt.

PLATE 26

The double-leaf doorway is composed of two panels, the upper being the larger. Garlands decorate the spandrel. The fanlight has nine radiating spokes ending in arrowheads, with the construction date inscribed in the hub, AH 1292 (AD 1875).

▶ 6 Shari' al-'Umrani, off Shari' Bulaq al-Gadid. The house belonged to the heirs of al-Shaykh al-Badrawi.

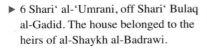

PLATE 27

▲ 11 'Ish al-Nakhl, Shari'
Bulaq al-Gadid, dates to the
third quarter of the nineteenth century.

▲ This entrance has a three-panel door, with the central
panel being the largest. The archivolt and door lintel
share the same plant motif. Garland ornamentation
adorns the spandrel.

PLATE 28

The double-leaf doors have three panels. The spokes of the wrought-iron fanlight end in double circles. The archivolt is unusual in its undulating motif. The entablature consists of two intricately decorated cornices, the lower with an entrelac motif and the upper with two rows of *muqarnasat*.

▶ 4 Shari' al-Wasti, Bulaq. The building belonged to the heirs of 'Ali Abu Nigm al-Gayar. Note the large, rectangular windows have been made smaller.

PLATE 29

▲ 29 Darb al-Habbala, Midan
al-Sayyida 'Aysha.

▶ The original door has been replaced by
a twentieth-century door, but the
entrance is of nineteenth-century
design. The archivolt has entrelac ornamentation and the spandrel has garland
motifs. Three rows of *muqarnasat* decorate the entablature. Bearing the year
of construction, AH 1292 (AD 1875), the
nine-spoke fanlight ends with either an
arrowhead or a star and crescent.

PLATE 30

The fanlight is in nine-
teenth-century style and
the original door was
replaced by a twentieth-
century-style door. The
archivolt has undulating
motifs and the spandrel is
adorned with arabesque
ornamentation.

3 Darb al-Dalil, al-Darb al-Ahmar,
dates to the 1890s.

PLATE 31

▲ 6 Harat al-Shadhliya, Bab al-Nasr, dates to the 1890s.

▲ The double-leaf doorway's upper panel is decorated with quadrangled motifs and the lower panel with *ma'kali* ornamentation.

PLATE 32

The spandrel is unique, containing three decorative friezes of plant motifs and fruits in the shape of a bunch of grapes. The entablature comprises a triple row of *muqarnasat*.

▶ 15 Harat Birguwan, al-Gamaliya. Dated to the late nineteenth or early twentieth century, this house was owned by Mustafa Bey al-Nagdi.

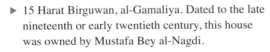

PLATE 33

▲ 5 Harat Abu 'Uf, Darb al-Husr, al-
Khalifa, dates to the late nineteenth
or early twentieth century.

▲ The lower panel of the double-leaf door has a
pyramidal inlay. The entrance's upper part is
without decoration.

PLATE 34

◄ The keystone is adorned with plant motifs and the upper part of the entrance is not elaborately decorated.

▶ 27 Midan Salah al-Din, al-Qal'a. Dated to the early twentieth century, this property was owned by al-Shaykh Muhammad Khalaf.

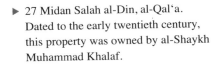

PLATE 35

▲ 18 Harat al-Khawas, Shari' al-Bayumi,
dates to the early twentieth century.
The wooden bays are characteristic of
the neo-Islamic architectural style of
old Cairo.

▲ In this double-leaf doorway, the door panel's
inner frieze has wood-carved decorative motifs.
The upper part of the entrance is undecorated.

PLATE 36

◄ This house has a unique stone doorway. The horseshoe fanlight is made of wrought iron in a grid pattern with three *mufruka* design elements. Above the archivolt is an opening in the shape of a *mihrab* with columns on either side. The entablature comprises a triple row of *muqarnasat*.

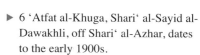

▶ 6 'Atfat al-Khuga, Shari' al-Sayid al-Dawakhli, off Shari' al-Azhar, dates to the early 1900s.

PLATE 37

▲ 37 'Abud al-Zumur, Midan al-Giza,
dates to the 1930s.

▲ The stone doorway's archivolt comprises a row
of *muqarnasat* framed by a *mima* motif. The
entablature and the arch spring have two rows of
muqarnasat. Two bosses decorate the spandrel.

PLATE 38

This double-leaf door is made of wood and comprises four panels. The second panel from the top and the lowest panel have *ma'kali* ornamentation, while the large central panel has hexagonal ornamentation. The fanlight has an elegant *maymuni* character. The entrance is adorned with pendant *muqarnasat* and the pilaster is embellished with geometrical motifs.

▶ 13 Shari' Kanisat al-Rum al-Kathulik, al-Faggala. Dated November 1910, this building was owned by Ghali Effendi Nakhla.

PLATE 39

▲ 13 Shari' al-Hud, off Shari' al-Bayumi.
This property was owned by Musa
Salim al-Gazzar.

▶ This is a particularly beautiful wooden
double-leaf doorway whose lower panels
are decorated with octagonal star-plate
ornamentations. Inscribed on the lintel is
Idkhuluha bi-salamin aminin ('Enter in
peace and security'), and the date of construction, AH 1345. The keystone is also
inscribed with the construction date,
AD 1925.

PLATE 40

◀ 5 Darb Husayn, Midan al-Gaysh. Dated 1910–1917, this was the property of the heirs of al-Hagg Muhammad al-Bur'i.

▲ Detail of the upper section of the doorway, showing the ornate stucco decorations. In the pilaster, a diamond shape encloses a four-petaled flower with six-petaled flowers at each corner. The spandrel has an arabesque motif with a six-pointed star in the center.

▶ This unique neo-Islamic
entrance was later
changed to become a
room with a window.
The entablature consists
of various cornices. The
lower one has entrelac
decoration and three
decorated bosses.

PLATE 41

The neo-Islamic doorway is in the shape of a *mihrab*. The whole door is made of wrought iron, each leaf having two parts: the upper part bearing hexagonal motifs in two sizes, the smaller ones surrounding six-pointed stars. The lower part is decorated with an octagonal star-plate. The archivolt and the top of the entrance are surrounded by *jift* and *mima* motifs.

▶ 100 Shari' 26 July. Dated 1920, the property was owned by Girgis Salih.

PLATE 42

▲ 1 Shari' Sidi al-Khutari,
off Shari' 26 July. Dated
1910–1917, this house
belonged to Salih
Muhammad al-'Irqsusi.

▲ This neo-Islamic style doorway takes the shape of a
mihrab. The upper section of the leaf (two-thirds of the
door length) is made of wrought iron with hexagonal
motifs and six-pointed stars in two different sizes. The
lower section has star-plate ornamentation. The spandrel
has an arabesque motif surrounded by *jift* and *mima* motifs.

PLATE 43

◄ This rather eclectic doorway has European-style decoration on the wrought-iron door. The entablature has four units of triple-rowed *muqarnasat*. The upper part of the pilaster comprises two columns ending with two units of double-rowed *muqarnasat*.

▶ 13 Shari' al-'Aziz, off Shari' al-Zuhur, Shubra, dates to the 1920s.

PLATE 44

▲ 2 Harat Ra'uf, Shari' al-Shaykh al-Baghal, off Shari' Zayn al-'Abdin. Dated 1918–1925, this was the property of Muhammad Effendi Nur.

▲ The door is made entirely of wrought iron with European-style decoration, while the stone entrance has the traditional Islamic-style curved lintel. The keystone, spandrels, and upper part of the pilaster are decorated with Islamic motifs.

PLATE 45

This neo-Islamic-style doorway has inscribed on its lintel the Qur'anic verse, *Wa atu al-buyut min abwabiha wa itaqu Allah la'allakum tuflihun* (Surat al-Baqara 189: 'Enter houses through the proper doors. And fear Allah, that you may prosper'). The entablature consists of pendant *muqarnasat* and the entire entrance is surrounded by *jift* and *mima* motifs. Two columns stand on either side of the entrance with room made for a small bench. The upper part of the door leaf is in the shape of a *mihrab*. Two rows of *muqarnasat* decorate the plate-band. The lower section of the door leaf has two octagonal star-plates in two sizes, the smaller fitting inside the larger.

▶ 96 Shari' 26 July. Dated 1921, this was the property of Salih Effendi Haggag al-Zayni.

PLATE 46

▲ 3 Harat Khukhat al-Samni, Shari'
Bulaq al-Gadid. Dated 1910–1917,
this property belonged to al-Mu'allim
Khamis and his wife Zaynab.

▲ In this neo-Islamic doorway, the wrought-iron upper
section takes the form of hexagonal motifs and six-
pointed stars. The lintel is inscribed with a poem in
Arabic calligraphy; the first verse reads, *wa
ja'alnaha tuhfa li-l-nazirin* ('We have created it to be
a marvel to see'). Pendant *muqarnasat* decorate the
upper part of the entrance, and the pilaster and lintel
area are surrounded by *jift* and *mima* motifs.

PLATE 47

◀ Star-plates decorate the lower section of the door leaves. The door lintel has two rows of *muqarnasat*. The wrought-iron work in the two-part fanlight takes a similar form to that of the door's upper section.

▶ 5 Harat al-Qirabiya, Bab Zuwayla. Dated January 1906, this building was constructed for al-Hagg Hassan Muhammad Silim. Note the woodwork façade characteristic of old Cairo's neo-Islamic architecture of the early twentieth century.

PLATE 48

▲ 20, Shariʻ al-Sayyid al-Dawakhli, al-Azhar, dates to the early 1900s.

▶ In this neo-Islamic doorway, the upper section of the door leaf is in the shape of a *mihrab* with marvelous geometrical, wrought-iron motifs. Three rows of *muqarnasat* decorate the plate-band area. Octagonal star-plates in two sizes, the smaller within the larger, adorn the lower section of the door. The door's threshold is decorated with slender triangles fitting inside one another.

PLATE 49

◀ The upper section of this neo-Islamic doorway is surrounded by a *jift* and *mima* motif. The wrought-iron, upper leaf section is shaped in large, four-sided motifs. A double row of *muqarnasat* decorates the door lintel. A *jift* and scissors motif decorates the door's cornice. The lower section of the door has mixed-shape *ma'kali* ornamentation.

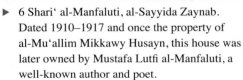

▶ 6 Shari' al-Manfaluti, al-Sayyida Zaynab. Dated 1910–1917 and once the property of al-Mu'allim Mikkawy Husayn, this house was later owned by Mustafa Lutfi al-Manfaluti, a well-known author and poet.

PLATE 50

▲ 7 al-Darb al-Asfar, al-Gamaliya,
dated 1910–1917, belonged to
Hassan Effendi al-Mufti.

▶ This neo-Islamic doorway has a
straight lintel of projecting voussoirs. The upper section of the
door leaf has small, four-sided
motifs of wrought iron. The
plate-band area has two rows of
muqarnasat between two corbels
that also have two rows of
muqarnasat. The door lintel is
decorated with a double row of
muqarnasat.

PLATE 51

A crescent shapes the center of this neo-Islamic door's upper section. An octagonal star-plate decorates the lower section of the door. The door lintel includes twelve units of triple-rowed *muqarnasat*, while the plate-band is adorned with six units of triple-rowed *muqarnasat*.

▶ 14 Darb al-Masmat, al-Gamaliya. Dated 1910–1917, this property was owned by al-Sayyid 'Arafa al-Husayni.

PLATE 56

▲ 14 Shari' al-Gami' al-Isma'ili,
al-Nasriya. Dated to 1910–1917,
this property belonged to the
heirs of Muhammad Effendi
Ratib al-Hakim.

▲ This doorway was constructed to express the
owner's nationalist sentiment. The door leaf's
upper wrought-iron section combines crescent and
snake-head motifs. The kinetic snake-head form
also appears in the two-part fanlight.

PLATE 57

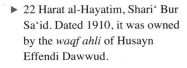

◀ Circular wrought iron strips constitute the decorative units predominating in the upper section of the door and fanlight. Crescent and snake head and tail motifs decorate the upper section of the door leaf. The fanlight has eight semiclosed snake-head motifs and at its center a six-petaled flower enclosed in a circle.

▶ 22 Harat al-Hayatim, Shari' Bur Sa'id. Dated 1910, it was owned by the *waqf ahli* of Husayn Effendi Dawwud.

PLATE 58

▲ 33 Harat al-Za'farana, Shari' Bur
Sa'id, dated 1910.

▲ The doorway has a curved lintel and projecting keystone. The upper section of the door leaf and the
two-part fanlight carry the combination of snake head
and tail, and crescent motifs that were the artistic
expression of nationalism at the time.

PLATE 59

◀ Having a straight lintel, this unusual doorway is highly embellished. The upper part of the door leaf has four snake-head motifs, two facing each other and two in opposite directions. Four snake-head motifs decorate the two-part fanlight.

▶ 8 Harat 'Agami, Shari' al-'Adawiya al-Barani, Bulaq, dates to the 1920s.

PLATE 60

▲ 2 Harat 'Abdallah 'Ezzat, Shari'
Muhammad Shakir, al-Hilmiya
al-Gadida. Dated November 15,
1910, this house was owned by
'Abdallah 'Ezzat Pasha.

▲ The snake-head motif is the predominant decorative unit in the upper section of the door leaf and
the two-part fanlight. Four intersecting snake-
head motifs adorn the arched upper section of the
door leaf.

PLATE 61

◀ A crescent of wrought iron decorates the upper door leaf section. Above the crescent are eight semiclosed snake tail strips. Below the crescent are two transverse iron strips ending in a snake tail and opposite one another. The entablature has eight units of double rowed *muqarnasat*. The keystone is in the shape of a royal emblem.

▶ 1 Harat Nada, Shari' al-Bayumi, dates to the 1930s.

PLATE 62

▲ 5 'Atfat Baha', Darb al-Magharba,
Bab al-Nasr, dates to the 1920s.

▶ At the center of the upper door leaf
section is a flower with two circles of
wrought iron, one inside the other. The
upper and lower thirds of this door leaf
contain snake-tail motifs taking several
forms. The entrance lintel comprises
a joggled voussoir and the upper door
jamb is decorated with an engraving
of a human figure inside a *mihrab*.

PLATE 63

▶ 4 Harat Rif'at, Shari'
Muhammad 'Ali, dates
to the 1930s.

◀ The fanlight, showing two
animated snakes in motion
facing one another, beside
other snake tails.

▶ Snake head and tail motifs taking several forms decorate the upper section of the door leaf. Another motif used is a flower inside a crescent. The door entrance is surrounded by two friezes, the outer one in the shape of open shells.

PLATE 64

◄ This entrance has a straight lintel with projecting keystone and a door in the art nouveau style. The snake tail motif is the dominant decorative motif in the fanlight and upper door leaf section. The lower section is in the form of a sun disk with longitudinal bands representing the sun's rays.

▶ 6 Harat Tamim al-Rasafi, al-Sayyida Zaynab, dates to the 1920s.

PLATE 65

▲ 7 Shari' al-Wasti, Bulaq,
dates to the 1920s.

▲ The entrance lintel of this art nouveau-style doorway consists
of joggled voussoirs. The lower door leaf section is in the
shape of a sun disk.

PLATE 66

◄ A projecting keystone and straight lintel shape this building's stone entrance. Snake head and tail motifs adorn the fanlight. Intricate wrought iron decorates the upper section of the door leaf.

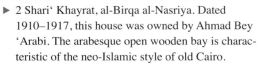

▶ 2 Shari' Khayrat, al-Birqa al-Nasriya. Dated 1910–1917, this house was owned by Ahmad Bey 'Arabi. The arabesque open wooden bay is characteristic of the neo-Islamic style of old Cairo.

PLATE 67

▲ 1 'Atfat al-Nidi, Shari' Bur
Sa'id, Darb al-Gamamiz, dates
to the 1920s.

▲ This straight-lintel entrance has a unique stucco garland
pediment. Snake head and tail motifs of different shapes
adorn the upper door leaf section.

PLATE 68

This entrance has a Greco-Roman pediment and straight lintel. Engraved plant motifs decorate the lower door leaf section.

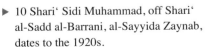
10 Shari' Sidi Muhammad, off Shari' al-Sadd al-Barrani, al-Sayyida Zaynab, dates to the 1920s.

PLATE 69

▲ 17 Harat al-Subqi, Ard al-Tawil,
Shubra, dates to the early 1900s.

▲ A Greco-Roman pediment and straight lintel dis-
tinguish this door entrance. The two-part fanlight
is adorned with special circular motifs.

PLATE 70

◄ This art nouveau curved-lintel doorway has a two-leaf door whose upper section contains wrought-iron decorations.

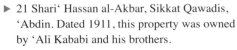

▶ 21 Shari' Hassan al-Akbar, Sikkat Qawadis, 'Abdin. Dated 1911, this property was owned by 'Ali Kababi and his brothers.

PLATE 71

▲ 8 Nasr al-Din al-Shaykh, Shari' 26 July, dates to the 1930s. It was recently demolished.

▲ This doorway is festooned with two stucco cornices. The inner one comprises a five-petaled flower motif surrounding the upper part of the door.

PLATE 72

Arabesque decorations adorn the entrance lintel and the upper part of the pilaster. A row of corbels graces the entablature. Snake-tail motifs are fashioned in the wrought iron of the door leaf and fanlight.

17 Shari' Wabur al-Faransawi, off Shari' 26 July. Dated to 1910–1917, this house belonged to the heirs of Muhammad 'Arafa.

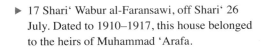

PLATE 73

▲ 7 Harat Zuhni, Birkat al-Fil, al-Sayyida Zaynab. Dated to 1910–1917, this was the property of the heirs of 'Ali Pasha Sirri.

▲ Lavish wrought-iron work embellishes the upper door leaf section and fanlight. Four sets of pyramids make up the lower section of the door leaf.

PLATE 74

This curved-lintel entrance is surrounded by a pilaster with circular bosses. The upper door leaf section comprises a grid of wrought iron circles. A double row of *muqarnasat* shapes the plate-band area.

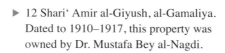

▶ 12 Shari' Amir al-Giyush, al-Gamaliya. Dated to 1910–1917, this property was owned by Dr. Mustafa Bey al-Nagdi.

PLATE 79

▲ 13 Shari' Qasr al-Lu'lu'a,
al-Faggala, dated 1910.

▲ The entrance has straight lintel and projecting keystone.
The door is in the art nouveau style. The lower door leaf
section is engraved with a flower basket.

PLATE 80

The upper section of the door leaf is carved in the shape of birds surrounded by plant motifs. The large central section contains a hexagonal flower inside a circle, along with two other flowers in the upper and lower parts. The two-part fanlight has the same motif found in the central section.

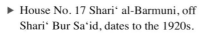

▶ House No. 17 Shari' al-Barmuni, off Shari' Bur Sa'id, dates to the 1920s.

PLATE 81

▶ 9 'Atfat al-Ballah, Shari' al-
Bayumi, dates to the 1920s. The
house has been demolished with
the exception of the ground floor
and its doorway. The stone
entrance has a straight lintel. The
upper door-leaf section is engraved
with a flower basket and other
plant motifs. This door has a distinctive plate-band area decorated
by two corbels, an arch surrounding a human face, and plant motifs.

PLATE 82

▲ Early twentieth-century architecture in old Cairo: woodwork elements in the façade
of 2 'Atfat al-Bassas, off Shari' al-Banhawi, Bab al-Nasr.

PLATE 83

▶ Early twentieth-century architecture in old Cairo: four open woodwork projections on 8 Darb al-Husr, off Shari' al-Ashraf, al-Khalifa (now demolished).

PLATE 84

▲ Early twentieth-century architecture in old Cairo: four closed woodwork projections on 2 Darb al-Shaykh al-Sayyim, off Shari' al-Banhawi, Bab al-Nasr.

PLATE 85

▲ Early twentieth-century architecture in old Cairo: two closed
woodwork projections on 29 'Atfat al-Shaykh 'Abd al-Latif,
Harat al-Mabyada, al-Gamaliya.

PLATE 86

◄ Early twentieth-century
architecture in old Cairo:
closed woodwork projec-
tions on 1 Darb Azuz,
ʻAtfat al-Halla, off Shariʻ
al-Bayumi, al-Husayniya.

▶ **8**

Height/Width	320 x 140 cm
Leaf of door	240 x 70 cm
Upper panel	44 x 42 cm
Middle panel	90 x 42 cm
Lower panel	44 x 42 cm
Jamb	20 cm
Pilaster	30 cm

▶ **9**

Height/Width	295 x 120 cm
Leaf of door	220 x 60 cm
Upper panel	100 x 46 cm
Lower panel	46 x 46 cm
Jamb	25 cm
Pilaster	50 cm

▶ **10**

Height/Width	295 x 170 cm
Leaf of door	140 x 85 cm
Jamb	25 cm
Pilaster	40 cm

▶ **11** (PTR 1902–1909 no. 11573/237/32, p. 84)

Height/Width	340 x 150 cm
Leaf of door	250 x 75 cm
Jamb	30 cm
Pilaster	50 cm

► **12** (PTR 1910–1917 no. 11972/256/32, p. 84)

Height/Width	350 x 140 cm
Leaf of door	250 x 70 cm
Upper panel	100 x 46 cm
Lower panel	46 x 46 cm
Jamb	25 cm
Pilaster	50 cm

► **13** (PTR 1910–1917 no. 11236/245/32, p. 30)

Height/Width	305 x 132 cm
Leaf of door	230 x 65 cm
Jamb	25 cm
Pilaster	40 cm

► **14** (PTR 1910–1917 no. 10315/208/32, p. 2)

Height/Width	290 x 110 cm
Leaf of door	220 x 55 cm
Jamb	22 cm
Pilaster	33 cm

► **15**

Height/Width	310 x 150 cm
Leaf of door	245 x 75 cm
Upper panel	101 x 50 cm
Middle panel	35 x 50 cm
Lower panel	65 x 50 cm
Jamb	25 cm
Pilaster	50 cm

▶ **16** (PTR 1902–1909 no. 12432/258/32, p. 192)

Height/Width	410 x 210
Leaf of door	310 x 105
Jamb	20 cm

▶ **17** (PTR 1902–1909 no. 11584/238/32, p. 89)

Height/Width	304 x 166 cm
Jamb	18 cm
Pilaster	40 cm

▶ **18** (PTR 1902–1909 no. 5166/95/32, p. 187)

Height/Width	405 x 210 cm
Leaf of door	275 x 105 cm
Upper panel	140 x 84 cm
Lower panel	60 x 84 cm
Jamb	50 cm
Pilaster	50 cm

▶ **19**

Height/Width	325 x 130 cm
Leaf of door	245 x 130 cm
Jamb	27 cm
Pilaster	27 cm

▶ **20** (PTR 1902–1909 no. 5186/96/32, p. 129)

Height/Width	280 x 130 cm
Jamb	25 cm
Pilaster	30 cm

► **21** (PTR 1910–1917 no. 5748/107/32, p. 42)

Height/Width	425 x 204 cm
Leaf of door	295 x 102 cm
Upper panel	140 x 83 cm
Lower panel	83 x 83 cm
Jamb	50 cm
Pilaster	50 cm

► **22** (PTR 1910–1917 no. 5747/107/32, p. 88)

Height/Width	315 x 130 cm
Leaf of door	245 x 65 cm
Jamb	25 cm
Pilaster	50 cm

► **23** (PTR 1910–1917 no. 5748/107/32, p. 15)

Height/Width	360 x 155 cm
Leaf of door	250 x 155 cm
Jamb	25 cm
Pilaster	50 cm

► **24**

Height/Width	340 x 130 cm
Leaf of door	240 x 65 cm
Upper panel	140 x 45 cm
Lower panel	57 x 45 cm
Jamb	40 cm
Pilaster	40 cm

▶ **25**

Height/Width	370 x 140 cm
Leaf of door	260 x 70 cm
Jamb	40 cm

▶ **26** (PTR 1910–1917 no. 5840/111/32, p. 32)

Height/Width	350 x 130 cm
Leaf of door	270 x 65 cm
Upper panel	128 x 48 cm
Lower panel	48 x 48 cm
Jamb	27 cm
Pilaster	50 cm

▶ **27** (PTR 1910–1917 no. 5840/110/32, p. 45)

Height/Width	370 x 170 cm
Leaf of door	275 x 85 cm
Upper panel	33 x 57 cm
Middle panel	145 x 57 cm
Lower panel	33 x 57 cm
Jamb	25 cm
Pilaster	55 cm

▶ **28** (PTR 1910–1917 no. 5832/110/32, p. 28)

Height/Width	400 x 180 cm
Leaf of door	290 x 90 cm
Upper panel	48 x 60 cm
Middle panel	104 x 60 cm
Lower panel	67 x 60 cm
Jamb	30 cm
Pilaster	50 cm

► **29**

Height/Width	335 x 122 cm
Leaf of door	250 x 61 cm
Upper panel	116 x 42 cm
Lower panel	72 x 42 cm
Jamb	20 cm
Pilaster	28 cm

► **30**

Height/Width	350 x 150 cm
Leaf of door	270 x 75 cm
Upper panel	133 x 52 cm
Lower panel	55 x 52 cm
Jamb	25 cm
Pilaster	50 cm

► **31**

Height/Width	315 x 135 cm
Leaf of door	250 x 62 cm
Upper panel	101 x 46 cm
Cornice	17 x 48 cm
Lower panel	46 x 46 cm
Jamb	20 cm
Pilaster	50 cm

► **32** (PTR 1910–1917 no. 2649/45/32, p. 27)

Height/Width	340 x 150 cm
Leaf of door	250 x 75 cm
Upper panel	150 x 52 cm
Lower panel	70 x 52 cm
Jamb	18 cm
Pilaster	42 cm

▶ **33**

Height/Width	380 x 140 cm
Leaf of door	295 x 70 cm
Upper panel	137 x 50 cm
Lower panel	62 x 50 cm
Jamb	27 cm
Pilaster	50 cm

▶ **34** (PTR 1910–1917 no. 5840/111/32, p. 32)

Height/Width	375 x 150 cm
Leaf of door	275 x 75 cm
Upper panel	133 x 56 cm
Lower panel	54 x 56 cm
Jamb	50 cm cm

▶ **35** (PTR 1910–1917 no. 5840/110/32, p. 45)

Height/Width	330 x 130 cm
Leaf of door	265 x 62 cm
Upper panel	110 x 40 cm
Cornice	24 x 40 cm
Lower panel	62 x 40 cm
Jamb	25 cm
Pilaster	50 cm

▶ **36** (PTR 1910–1917 no. 5832/110/32, p. 28)

Height/Width	410 x 140 cm
Leaf of door	320 x 70 cm
Jamb	27 cm
Pilaster	53 cm

▶ **37**

Height/Width	420 x 150 cm
Leaf of door	270 x 75 cm

▶ **38** (PTR 1910–1917 no. 7867/155/32, p. 55)

Height/Width	370 x 170 cm
Leaf of door	330 x 85 cm

▶ **39** (PTR 1926–1933 no. 11354/232/32, p. 24)

Height/Width	360 x 140 cm
Leaf of door	260 x 70 cm
Upper panel	118 x 55 cm
Cornice	22 x 55 cm
Lower panel	55 x 55 cm

▶ **40** (PTR 1910–1917 no. 2665/45/32, p. 36)

Jamb	18 cm
Pilaster	36 cm

▶ **41** (PTR 1918–1925 no. 6020/114/32, p. 62)

Height/Width	460 x 190 cm
Upper section	200 x 95 cm
Lower section	100 x 95 cm

► **42** (PTR 1910–1917 no. 5758/107/32, p. 31)

Height/Width	360 x 150 cm
Upper section	225 x 56 cm
Cornice	63 x 13 cm
Lower section	72 x 56 cm

► **43**

Height/Width	390 x 165 cm
Leaf of door	310 x 80 cm
Upper section	240 x 80 cm
Lower panel	70 x 80 cm

► **44** (PTR 1918–1925 no. 13031/270/32, p. 42)

Height/Width	375 x 155 cm
Leaf of door	290 x 75 cm
Upper section	200 x 75 cm
Lower section	90 x 75 cm

► **45** (PTR 1918–1925 no. 8020/114/32, p. 62)

Height/Width	350 x 160 cm
Leaf of door	320 x 80 cm
Upper section	155 x 57 cm
Cornice	28 x 57 cm
Lower section	57 x 57 cm

▶ **46** (PTR 1910–1917 no. 5827/109/32, p. 64)

Height/Width	300 x 130 cm
Leaf of door	300 x 65 cm
Upper section	150 x 45 cm
Cornice	20 x 45 cm
Lower section	60 x 45 cm
Threshold	18 x 45 cm

▶ **47** (PTR 1902–1909 no. 9721/196/32, p. 75)

Height/Width	400 x 180 cm
Leaf of door	305 x 90 cm
Upper section	160 x 70 cm
Cornice	16 x 75 cm
Lower section	62 x 70 cm

▶ **48**

Height/Width	415 x 150 cm
Leaf of door	310 x 75 cm
Upper section	168 x 55 cm
Cornice	18 x 63 cm
Lower section	55 x 55 cm

▶ **49**

Height/Width	355 x 155 cm
Leaf of door	280 x 75 cm
Upper section	136 x 55 cm
Lower section	55 x 55 cm

▶ **50** (PTR 1910–1917 no. 15464/317/32, p. 39)

Height/Width	350 x 135 cm
Leaf of door	280 x 67 cm
Upper section	135 x 44 cm
Lower section	58 x 44 cm

▶ **51** (PTR 1910–1917 no. 15577/318/32, p. 45)

Height/Width	325 x 130 cm
Leaf of door	250 x 65 cm
Upper section	120 x 45 cm
Cornice	20 x 50 cm
Lower section	65 x 45 cm

▶ **52** (PTR 1910–1917 no. 14054/290/32, p. 38)

Height/Width	325 x 160 cm
Leaf of door	275 x 80 cm
Upper section	130 x 55 cm
Cornice	18 x 62 cm
Lower section	55 x 55 cm

▶ **53** (PTR 1910–1917 no. 5757/107/32, p. 57)

Height/Width	305 x 140 cm
Leaf of door	240 x 70 cm
Upper section	130 x 54 cm
Cornice	23 x 54 cm
Lower section	54 x 54 cm

▶ **54** (PTR 1910–1917 no. 15487/317/32, p. 48)

Height/Width	370 x 130 cm
Leaf of door	270 x 65 cm
Upper section	125 x 50 cm
Cornice	22 x 55 cm
Lower section	56 x 50 cm

▶ **55** (PTR 1910–1917 no. 11964/246/32, p. 76)

Height/Width	350 x 130 cm
Leaf of door	255 x 65 cm
Upper section	97 x 47 cm
Cornice	12 x 55 cm
Lower section	72 x 47 cm

▶ **56** (PTR 1910–1917 no. 12998/269/32, p. 82)

Height/Width	375 x 140 cm
Leaf of door	265 x 70 cm
Upper section	150 x 50 cm
Cornice	22 x 50 cm
Lower section	50 x 50 cm

▶ **57** (PTR 1910–1917 no. 12943/268/32, p. 81)

Height/Width	355 x 130 cm
Leaf of door	270 x 65 cm
Upper section	142 x 45 cm
Cornice	14 x 49 cm
Lower section	65 x 45 cm

► **58** (PTR 1910–1917 no. 13010/270/32, p. 88)

Height/Width	355 x 135 cm
Leaf of door	290 x 67 cm
Upper section	152 x 35 cm
Cornice	17 x 42 cm
Lower section	72 x 35 cm

► **59**

Height/Width	350 x 144 cm
Leaf of door	260 x 72 cm
Upper section	90 x 45 cm
Lower section	45 x 45 cm

► **60** (PTR 1910–1917 no. 11950/245/32, p. 6)

Height/Width	380 x 150 cm
Leaf of door	285 x 75 cm
Upper section	145 x 56 cm
Lower section	56 x 66 cm

► **61**

Height/Width	350 x 160 cm
Leaf of door	255 x 80 cm
Upper section	138 x 62 cm
Cornice	14 x 62 cm
Lower section	72 x 62 cm

► **62**

Height/Width	340 x 150 cm
Leaf of door	275 x 75 cm
Upper section	140 x 48 cm
Lower section	55 x 46 cm

► **63**

Height/Width	340 x 130 cm
Leaf of door	270 x 65 cm
Upper section	136 x 46 cm
Cornice	13 x 46 cm
Lower section	65 x 46 cm

► **64**

Height/Width	360 x 160 cm
Leaf of door	295 x 80 cm
Upper section	150 x 48 cm
Lower section	75 x 48 cm

► **65**

Height/Width	310 x 120 cm
Leaf of door	310 x 60 cm
Upper section	172 x 43 cm
Lower section	65 x 43 cm

► **66** (PTR 1910–1917 no. 13000/270/32, p. 15)

Height/Width	410 x 150 cm
Leaf of door	290 x 75 cm
Upper section	152 x 50 cm
Cornice	20 x 50 cm
Lower section	50 x 50 cm

► **67**

Height/Width	320 x 120 cm
Leaf of door	255 x 60 cm
Upper section	130 x 45 cm
Lower section	60 x 45 cm

► **68**

Height/Width	355 x 155 cm
Leaf of door	280 x 77 cm
Upper section	136 x 55 cm
Lower section	55 x 55 cm

► **69**

Height/Width	330 x 140 cm
Leaf of door	260 x 70 cm
Upper section	120 x 47 cm
Middle section	32 x 47 cm
Lower section	50 x 47 cm

► **70** (PTR 1910–1917 no. 7133/139/32, p. 96)

Height/Width	400 x 130 cm
Leaf of door	305 x 65 cm
Upper section	150 x 47 cm
Cornice	22 x 47 cm
Lower section	95 x 47 cm

► **71**

Height/Width	400 x 160 cm
Leaf of door	290 x 80 cm
Upper section	165 x 85 cm
Lower section	58 x 58 cm

► **72** (PTR 1910–1917 no. 5804/109/32, p. 11)

Height/Width	350 x 140 cm
Leaf of door	280 x 70 cm
Upper section	136 x 50 cm
Lower section	70 x 50 cm

► **73** (PTR 1910–1917 no. 13008/270/32, p. 42)

Height/Width	360 x 150 cm
Leaf of door	270 x 75 cm
Upper section	115 x 50 cm
Cornice	23 x 50 cm
Lower section	50 x 50 cm

▶ **74** (PTR 1910–1917 no. 2648/45/32, p. 91)

Height/Width	367 x 155 cm
Leaf of door	367 x 78 cm
Upper section	195 x 50 cm
Cornice	24 x 54 cm
Lower section	65 x 50 cm

▶ **75** (PTR 1910–1917 no. 16140/332/32, p. 20)

Height/Width	370 x 140 cm
Leaf of door	295 x 70 cm
Upper section	150 x 52 cm
Lower section	70 x 52 cm

▶ **76** (PTR 1918–1925 no. 9058/180/32, p. 30)

Height/Width	330 x 150 cm
Leaf of door	275 x 75 cm
Upper section	128 x 55 cm
Lower section	70 x 55 cm

▶ **77** (PTR 1910–1917 no. 8919/176/32, p. 94)

Height/Width	320 x 130 cm
Leaf of door	290 x 65 cm
Upper section	132 x 45 cm
Cornice	17 x 45 cm
Lower section	77 x 45 cm

► **78**

Height/Width	380 x 165 cm
Leaf of door	300 x 83 cm
Upper section	105 x 60 cm
Lower section	60 x 55 cm

► **79** (PTR 1910–1917 no. 7868/155/32, p. 41)

Height/Width	340 x 120 cm
Leaf of door	260 x 60 cm

► **80**

Height/Width	350 x 155 cm
Leaf of door	270 x 75 cm
Upper section	120 x 55 cm

► **81**

Height/Width	330 x 135 cm
Leaf of door	250 x 62 cm
Upper section	127 x 41 cm
Cornice	16 x 44 cm
Lower section	57 x 44 cm

GLOSSARY

arabesque: a complex design of interlocking floral, foliage, or geometrical patterns characteristic of Islamic art.

arch spring: the lowest supporting stones in an arch.

architrave: the lowermost member of a classical entablature, originally resting upon columns.

archivolt: a curved molding decorating the face of an arch.

'atfat (**or** *'atfa*): a closed alley.

boss: a round projecting decorative element in a stone wall.

corbel: a bracket, usually of stone (in pre–nineteenth-century architecture) or wood (in Rumi-style architecture); found in the plate-band area of the double-leaf doors of the twentieth century.

cornerstone: triangular area between two arches or between an arch and a wall; also called the spandrel.

cornice: raised wood molding between the upper and lower sections of double-leaf doors where the door handle is affixed; also the uppermost part of an entablature.

darb: a short and closed alley.

entablature: the part of an edifice above the columns, consisting of the architrave, frieze, and cornice.

entrelac: a decoration consisting of geometrically interlaced plant expressions.

fanlight: a window over a door or another window, often taking the form of a semicircle.

frieze: decorative band on an outside wall or border bearing lettering or sculpture.

gama'iya: an old method of assembling doors by connecting small, comb-shaped wood pieces without the use of glue or nails.

garland: a decoration combining leaves, flowers, and fruits or taking the shape of festoons.

harat (**or** *hara*): an alley.

hashwa (**pl.** *hashawat*): small wood pieces of various shapes and sizes used in forming a door panel.

jamb: the side or abutment of a door.

jift: widespread Islamic decorative units of two parallel bars ending in either a *mima* or a scissor motif.

keystone: the central stone at the top of an arch.

khukhat (**or** *khukha*): a narrow passage between two alleys.

leaf: a hinged or otherwise movable section of a folding door, shutter, or gate.

lintel: an architectural member, such as a beam or stone, supporting the weight above the door.

ma'kali: wood decoration consisting of vertical and horizontal rectangular pieces enclosing a square piece in the center.

mashrabiya: an oriel screened by latticework and supported by brackets or corbels.

maymuni: a method of assembling *mashrabiya* or windows by connecting small pieces of wood in a dovetail technique, without the used of glue or nails.

midan: an open area or plaza in a city or town, formed by the meeting or intersecting of two or more streets; a square.

mihrab: a recess in the wall of a mosque pointing toward the direction of Mecca; widely used in neo-Islamic architecture for the shape of the door or the upper leaf section.

mima: Islamic decoration taking the circular shape of the Arabic letter *mim*.

mufruka: wood decoration of the door panels having a square piece of wood with four radiating bars; in the twentieth century it is also made of wrought iron and widely used as a decorative unit in doors.

muqarnas (pl. *muqarnasat*): a decorative beehive-shaped unit used in Islamic architecture since the Fatimid era.

palmette: a plant leaf adapted decoratively and used in many artistic works.

panel: a framed board or plane.

pediment: a triangular gable of stone or bricks in the upper part of the entrance.

pilaster: a masonry stand that serves more of a decorative than an architectural function; generally flat and extending somewhat from the wall plane.

pivot: short shaft or fulcrum in either the lintel or the threshold of the entrance where the two projections of the stiles of the pre–nineteenth-century doorway are affixed.

plate-band: the area above the upper section of the door leaf.

rails: horizontal framing member in a door or a section of paneling.

shari': a street or roadway.

shura'a: the upper wrought-iron section of twentieth-century double-leaf doors.

shurfa (pl. *shurafat*): any set of crenels of various shapes and openings forming the top of the wall, widely used in Islamic architecture as decorative units.

sikkat (**or** *sikka*): a passage between two alleys.

stiles: the vertical boards that frame part of a door panel or window.

threshold: the stone, wood, or metal strip below a door or window.

triglyph: a decoration consisting of three grooves.

waqf: a religious endowment.

waqf ahli: a trust to benefit the family members of the donor and his or her descendants.

voussoir: a wedge-shaped stone or bricks used with others to construct an arch or vault.